CONTENTS

Bridge Technique Series

BRIDGE TECHNIQUE SERIES

TRICKS WITH FINESSES

David Bird • Marc Smith

MASTER POINT PRESS • TORONTO

Master Point Press
331 Douglas Ave
Toronto, Ontario, Canada
M5M 1H2
(416) 781-0351   Internet www.masterpointpress.com

Canadian Cataloguing in Publication Data
Bird, David, 1946-
Tricks with finesses

(Bridge technique; 12)
ISBN 1-894154-36-3

1. Contract bridge — Dummy play. I. Smith, Marc, 1960- .II Title.
III. Series: Bird, David, 1946-. Bridge technique; 12

GV1282.435.B57318 2001   795. 41'.53   C00-933105-0

Cover design and Interior: Olena S. Sullivan
Editor: Ray Lee

Printed and bound in Canada by Webcom Limited

1 2 3 4 5 6 7   07 06 05 04 03 02 01

Introduction

You can rarely make your contract simply by cashing top winners. To develop extra tricks, you will need to increase the power of your lesser cards. Often you will employ the finesse, one of the most important of all card play techniques.

Teachers have to fight with beginners to get them to take their first finesse. Once players see how a 'cheap' trick can be made, though, they become addicted to finessing. You may think that 'finessing' is hardly a worthwhile subject for a serious book on card play. After all, anyone can take a finesse — sometimes they win and sometimes they lose. What more is there to it?

If that is your view, we may have a surprise for you. In this book, you will find out which finesses to take and which ones to reject. You will discover which card should be led when finessing. We will look also at that perennial card play technique, timing. Do you always know when a particular finesse should be taken? And what about those awkward two-way finesses? Do you always guess them right? No — nor does anyone, but some players do so more often than most. Why is that?

Come with us as we explore these topics and many more. We begin with the simple question:

What is a finesse?

In raw terms, a finesse is an attempt to win a trick with a card that is not the highest remaining card in the suit (for example, the queen in an A-Q holding). The success or failure of a finesse depends on the position of the higher card, or cards, held by the defenders.

There are several common types of finesse. The first involves leading towards the lesser honor that you are hoping to score:

♣ A Q

♣ ???   [N / W E / S]   ♣ ???

♣ 3 2

You can always score one club trick with the ace. By leading towards dummy, and playing the queen if the king has not appeared, you can make a second club trick when West holds the king.

This is another example of the first type:

♢ K 2

♢ ???   [N / W E / S]   ♢ ???

♢ 4 3

You lead towards the king, the honor you are hoping to score. Once again, success will depend on the location of a particular card held by the defenders (the ace this time, the king in the first layout).

A second type of finesse involves leading a high card rather than a low one. The emphasis is more on 'trapping' the enemy high card:

♡ A 2

♡ ???   [N / W E / S]   ♡ ???

♡ Q J

You lead the queen from your hand and West's king (if he holds that card) is ambushed. You will score two heart tricks without loss.

In the next chapter, we will meet many more finesse positions as we examine how, why and when you should take a finesse. Those of you who had scant respect for the finesse as a technique may — reluctantly — have to change their opinion!

Some Finessing Techniques

We have already seen that you can score two tricks with small cards opposite an ace-queen combination simply by leading towards the ace-queen. Does it matter if the ace and queen are in separate hands?

```
             ♣ Q 5 3
              ┌─────┐
              │  N  │
♣ ? ? ?       │ W E │      ♣ ? ? ?
              │  S  │
              └─────┘
             ♣ A 4 2
```

Can you still take a finesse? Yes, by cashing the ace and then leading towards the queen you can establish a second club trick if West holds the king. Remember, you do not need to hold the master card in the suit in order to be able to finesse.

Indeed, you do not even have to cash the ace first — you can start by leading a low club towards dummy's queen. Doing things this way will cost a trick only on the rare occasions when East holds the singleton king of clubs.

However, be warned — the more cards you hold in the suit, the more likely a singleton king becomes. Suppose this is your trump suit:

```
             ♡ A Q 5 3
              ┌─────┐
              │  N  │
♡ ? ? ?       │ W E │      ♡ ? ? ?
              │  S  │
              └─────┘
             ♡ 9 7 6 4 2
```

You have nine cards in the suit now, so the chances of East holding a singleton king are dramatically higher. If you need to score five heart tricks, you will have to hope both that West holds the king and that the outstanding hearts are divided 2-2. Lead a heart from hand and finesse the queen. When your luck is in, the queen will win and both defenders will follow suit when you subsequently cash the ace.

Note that we said: 'if you need five heart tricks'. A recurring theme throughout this book will be to help you to determine when and if a finesse should be taken. The correct way to play a particular suit combination will often depend on how many tricks you need from that suit. Let's put the heart suit above into a full deal to see how you may be able to improve your chances via a safety play while still retaining the option of taking a finesse later.

```
              ♠ K Q 4
              ♡ A Q 5 3
              ♢ K 5
              ♣ 7 6 3 2
                    ┌─────────┐
                    │    N    │
  ♣ J led           │ W     E │
                    │    S    │
                    └─────────┘
              ♠ A J 9 5
              ♡ 9 7 6 4 2
              ♢ A Q 9
              ♣ A
```

You reach six hearts and West leads the jack of clubs to your ace. You could take a heart finesse at Trick 2. Doing so would bring home the contract more often than not. Even if the finesse lost, you would still be okay provided hearts broke evenly. Indeed, had you bid to seven hearts, leading to the queen on the first round would be correct. That's because you would need to play the trumps for no loser.

Playing in the small slam, you can afford to lose one heart trick. Losing two would be fatal, though. Can you see why it would be wrong to finesse the queen on the first round of hearts?

The answer is: because you would lose two tricks when East started with a singleton king. At Trick 2, you should lead a heart to the ace. This will reap instant benefit if East does happen to hold the singleton king. Suppose instead that both defenders follow to the ace of hearts but the king does not fall. If the remaining trumps are divided 1-1, you can make your contract simply by playing a second heart from dummy. That would be poor play, though. A much better idea is to re-enter your hand with a club ruff and lead a heart towards dummy's queen. Unless

East began with king third (when you could do nothing to stop him scoring two tricks), you will make your contract.

Timing was the key on this hand — by cashing the ace and leading towards the queen on the second round of trumps you still made your contract whenever West held the king of hearts. You succeeded also when East held the singleton king — increasing your chances by more than 6%.

This position is similar:

♠ A Q 10 7 3

N	
W	*E*
	S

♠ 8 5 4 2

Suppose this is your trump suit in a small slam and you can afford one loser but not two. If you finesse the queen and lose to the king, you may face an unpleasant guess on the second round. A finesse of the ten will win when West started with J-9-6; it will cost you the slam when West was dealt 9-6 and East K-J. You can avoid disasters of this sort by cashing the ace on the first round. You then return to your hand and lead towards the queen. By playing in this way, you hold your trump losers to one whenever it is possible to do so.

Entries and intermediates

In the situations we have looked at so far, there was only a single finesse to be taken. Often, though, you can finesse more than once in a suit — either repeating the same finesse or taking a different one. There are two factors that you must bear in mind when taking multiple finesses in a single suit — the number of entries you will need and whether you have sufficient intermediate cards to lead a high card for the finesse.

Let's start with an example where neither of these factors presents a problem:

♣ A 4 3 2

♣ ? ? ?

N	
W	*E*
	S

♣ ? ? ?

♣ Q J 10 9

Playing in a notrump contract, you need to score four club tricks.

That's easy enough — you can lead any of the cards from the South hand intending to run it unless West plays the king. By repeating the finesse until the king appears, you will score four tricks any time the king is in the West hand — a straight 50% chance.

Let's reduce the intermediate cards by just one spot:

$$\clubsuit \; A\,4\,3\,2$$

$$\clubsuit \; K\,9\,6\,5 \qquad \begin{array}{c} N \\ W \quad E \\ S \end{array} \qquad \clubsuit \; 7$$

$$\clubsuit \; Q\,J\,10\,8$$

You cannot make four club tricks now, even though the king is onside. With the suit dividing 4-1, your intermediates are not quite good enough. West will cover with his king at some stage and you will lose the fourth round of clubs to his nine.

Now let's see what effect the entry situation can have. Suppose, among your assets, you have this spade suit.

$$\spadesuit \; A\,Q\,J\,2$$

$$\spadesuit \; ??? \qquad \begin{array}{c} N \\ W \quad E \\ S \end{array} \qquad \spadesuit \; ???$$

$$\spadesuit \; 10\,5\,4\,3$$

The lead is in the South hand and you need four spade tricks. Unless you are clairvoyant and can 'see' that East holds a singleton king, your best chance is to finesse against West. Out of interest, what do you think the odds of scoring four tricks in this suit might be?

The answer depends on whether you have another entry to the South hand, in some different suit. Suppose first that you have no further entries. How would you go about scoring four tricks? Say you lead a low spade to the jack, which wins. Stuck in dummy, you will then be forced to lay down the ace and hope that West's king falls. The odds on the finesse itself were 50%, but this line of play needs to find West with either a singleton or doubleton king — not even 15%. Some difference, isn't it?

A better chance is to lead the ten of spades on the first round. By doing so, you hold the lead in the South hand should West choose not to cover. You ensure four spade tricks whenever West holds the king and the suit divides 3-2. That more than doubles your chances to 34%.

Can you see how to improve these odds further when you do have a side-suit entry to your hand?

With an outside entry, you would prefer not to expend the ten on the first round in case West holds a singleton king. (If you lead the ten on the first round, covered by West's king, East's ♠9-x-x-x will be promoted into a trick.) So, you lead low and finesse the jack. You can then return to hand to repeat the finesse. This line of play succeeds when the king is onside and either the suit splits 3-2 or West holds the singleton king. This gives you almost a 37% chance, which is the best you can do when you do not hold the ♠9.

The situation is exactly the same when your eight cards in a suit are divided 5-3:

```
                  ♡  J 3 2
                  ┌────────┐
                  │  N     │
   ♡  ? ? ?       │ W    E │      ♡  ? ? ?
                  │     S  │
                  └────────┘
                  ♡  A Q 10 5 4
```

Suppose you need all five heart tricks. With no outside entry to dummy, you must start by leading the jack, running it if East does not play the king. The lead will then remain in dummy for a second heart play, allowing you to pick up ♡K-x-x with East. When you have an outside entry to dummy you can again improve your prospects by leading a low card on the first round. This will also allow you to score five heart tricks when East holds a singleton king.

Even when you do hold adequate entries to both hands, there is one situation where you should lead an unsupported honor. That's when the defenders hold three cards including the king and ten:

```
                  ♠  J 8 3 2
                  ┌────────┐
                  │  N     │
   ♠  ? ? ?       │ W    E │      ♠  ? ? ?
                  │     S  │
                  └────────┘
                  ♠  A Q 9 7 6 5
```

The best chance of scoring six spade tricks is to take a finesse against East's presumed king. Suppose, first, that you lead low from dummy. East plays the four and you finesse with the queen. All will be well if West follows with the ten — your ace will drop East's king on the second round. Suppose, though, that West shows out on the first round. You will then lose a trick to East's remaining ♠K-10.

Starting with the jack from dummy cannot cost. If East covers with the king and West follows suit, then your queen will collect the only remaining spade. If, however, East covers and West discards, you will be able to re-enter dummy in a different suit and take a second-round finesse against East's remaining ♠ 10-4.

When you are uncertain whether or not to lead an honor for a finesse, ask yourself this question: will I be all right if the honor is covered? Here, you will be. In previous situations we saw that you could not afford a cover with a singleton king; it would promote a trick in the other defender's hand.

Now that you have the idea, here is a full deal on which you can test yourself. If you feel up to the challenge, cover the East-West hands and take over from declarer.

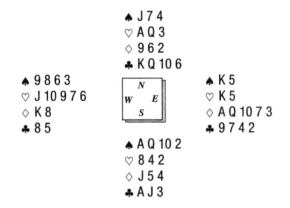

```
                    ♠ J 7 4
                    ♡ A Q 3
                    ◊ 9 6 2
                    ♣ K Q 10 6
 ♠ 9 8 6 3          ┌─────────┐      ♠ K 5
 ♡ J 10 9 7 6       │    N    │      ♡ K 5
 ◊ K 8              │  W   E  │      ◊ A Q 10 7 3
 ♣ 8 5              │    S    │      ♣ 9 7 4 2
                    └─────────┘
                    ♠ A Q 10 2
                    ♡ 8 4 2
                    ◊ J 5 4
                    ♣ A J 3
```

West leads the jack of hearts against your contract of 3NT. Firstly, are you tempted to take the heart finesse?

You shouldn't be. Even if it wins, you will still need to find the spade king onside. If the heart finesse loses, the defenders may switch to diamonds and you will go down even when four spade tricks were available. So, you rise with the ace of hearts at Trick 1 and must then concentrate on how to score four spade tricks. Any ideas?

Clearly, you need to find the king with East. As you do not have the nine of spades, it may seem that you also need the suit to break 3-3. Can you see how to improve on those rather meager odds?

In fact, you can make the contract when East holds the king of spades doubleton. What you must not do is to lead the jack of spades for the finesse. East will cover, holding a doubleton king, and West will then win the fourth round of the suit. Instead, lead a low spade and finesse (with either the ten or the queen). Now re-enter dummy with a club and lead dummy's second low spade. If the king does not appear on your right, you will finesse again and then lay down the ace of spades, hoping the suit was breaking 3-3 all along.

On the actual layout, East's king of spades pops up on the second round. Now it's a simple matter to win with the ace, cross to the jack of spades, return to hand with the ace of clubs, cash your fourth spade winner, and claim your contract with two high clubs in dummy.

On our next combination, you have all of the intermediate cards, but lack of an outside entry prevents you from scoring all of your apparent tricks:

```
                ◇ A Q J 10
                    N
◇ K 4 3 2       W       E       ◇ 5
                    S
                ◇ 9 8 7 6
```

Let's say the lead is in the South hand and you have one outside entry to your hand. You start by taking a winning finesse against West's king and return to hand using your outside entry. When you repeat the finesse, you again win the trick, but East discards. With no further entries to lead towards dummy's tenace, you cannot score a fourth diamond trick.

With all the high cards in dummy, this suit offered no flexibility. When dummy comes down with such a suit, you should be aware from the outset you cannot afford to waste entries to your hand. With that clue in mind, see how you tackle this deal:

```
                ♠ A K 8 4
                ♡ 7 5 4
                ◇ A Q J 10
                ♣ K 7
♠ J 9 5                         ♠ 6 2
♡ K Q 3         N               ♡ J 9 8 2
◇ K 9 6 2     W   E             ◇ 7 4
♣ J 6 4         S               ♣ Q 10 8 5 2
                ♠ Q 10 7 3
                ♡ A 10 6
                ◇ 8 5 3
                ♣ A 9 3
```

You bid unopposed to the ambitious spade slam and West leads the king of hearts, which you win with the ace. How would you continue?

To dispose of one of your heart losers, you will need four diamond tricks. If West holds king fourth you will need to lead diamonds three times from the South hand. This can be done only if you take an immediate diamond finesse at Trick 2. You can then draw trumps in three rounds, ending in your hand, and take a second diamond finesse. A club to the ace will allow you to repeat the winning finesse yet again, and the ◇A will provide a parking place for one of your heart losers.

On the final example in this section, you have all of the intermediate cards and the suit offers some flexibility. However, a lack of entries means that you must be careful:

♡ J 9 3 2

```
      N
  W       E
      S
```

♡ 7   ♡ K 8 6 5

♡ A Q 10 4

The lead is in dummy but there are no outside entries. How would you play to score four heart tricks, even if East holds king fourth?

First let's see what happens if you start by leading a low heart from dummy. That's no good as you will win the trick in hand. With no outside entry to dummy you will then be unable to repeat the winning finesse.

How about leading the jack? The jack wins the first round of the suit, allowing you to repeat the finesse, but when you win the second round of hearts in your hand West discards. With no further entry to dummy, you will again have to concede a trick to East's king.

Ah! Perhaps when you lead the jack from dummy you can play the ten underneath it? You can then lead the nine on the second round of hearts and the lead will remain in dummy for a third finesse.

It's not a bad idea, but there is a snag — East will cover the nine with his king on the second round of hearts. You will then be left with a losing heart and East's eight will win the fourth round of the suit.

Now observe the effect of leading the nine of hearts on the first round. You run the nine, following with the four from your hand. On the second round, you then lead the jack, and underplay with the ten, retaining the lead in dummy for a third finesse against East's king. Nor will it help East to cover either of the high leads from dummy since you have retained all of the honors in your hand.

Choosing the right type of finesse

How many tricks do you expect to take with this suit combination?

```
                ♣ A 4 3
                ┌─────────┐
                │    N    │
  ♣ ? ? ?       │ W     E │      ♣ ? ? ?
                │    S    │
                └─────────┘
                ♣ Q J 5 2
```

The best you can do is three, and even that is far from guaranteed. Many players mishandle the combination by leading the queen. Whether this runs to East's king, or is covered by the West's king and dummy's ace, you will score three tricks only when the suit breaks 3-3. That provides only a skinny 36% chance of making three tricks. Instead, you should cash the ace and lead twice towards the queen and jack. This will net three tricks whenever East holds the king (a 50% prospect), and also when West holds the king but the suit breaks 3-3 or when the king is singleton (a further 19%). So, by playing the suit correctly instead of incorrectly you bump your chances from 36% to 69%. What a massive difference!

You may recall that at the very start of this book we noted that there were two main types of finesse. In one you led towards the honor you were hoping to make (low towards the queen, here). In the other, you led an honor (the queen, here), knowing that you could kill the defender's covering honor. With a holding such as Q-J-10-x opposite A-x-x(-x) you can afford to play this second type of finesse. With only Q-J-x-x, you cannot. You are destined to lose at least one trick and may lose more if you lead the queen, playing the wrong type of finesse.

Having said all of that, there will be deals on which it would still be correct to run the queen with this suit combination. The best way to handle a single suit must always depend on the requirements of the hand as a whole. To illustrate this, let's put that club suit into a full deal:

```
              ♠ A 7
              ♡ 7 6 2
              ◇ A Q J 10 2
              ♣ A 4 3
♠ J 10 5 4        ┌─────┐        ♠ Q 9 6 3
♡ K Q 10 9 3      │  N  │        ♡ J 8 5
◇ 6               │W   E│        ◇ 8 5 4
♣ K 10 8          │  S  │        ♣ 9 7 6
                  └─────┘
              ♠ K 8 2
              ♡ A 4
              ◇ K 9 7 3
              ♣ Q J 5 2
```

You play in 3NT and West leads the ♡K. There are eight top tricks and you can easily develop a ninth trick in clubs by force. However, if you lose the lead the defenders may be able to cash enough heart winners to defeat your game. You must therefore aim to score your second club trick without relinquishing the lead.

In this instance, cashing the ♣A and leading towards your queen-jack would be the play of a complete bonehead. It would gain only on about 1.5% of hands (when East holds the king of clubs singleton). This time you need only two club tricks, not three, and you need them fast, without losing the lead. You should take the ace of hearts on the second round and lead the queen of clubs, intending to run it if West follows low.

As you see, the best play in a suit can depend on how many tricks you need. Needing two fast club tricks, you finesse against West. If you require three tricks, and can afford to lose the lead, finesse against East.

Should I cash a high card first?

Suppose the lead is in the North hand and you need four diamond tricks from this combination:

```
                  ◇ K 6 3 2
                  ┌─────┐
◇ ? ? ?           │  N  │        ◇ ? ? ?
                  │W   E│
                  │  S  │
                  └─────┘
                  ◇ A J 10 5
```

Other things being equal, you will play East for the missing queen. That's because you can pick up queen fourth in his hand but not in the

West hand. Should you cash the king before finessing the jack? Provided you have an outside entry to the North hand (to repeat the finesse), you should cash the king first. By doing so, you will pick up a singleton queen with West.

Suppose next that you do not have an outside entry to dummy. It would then be correct to finesse the jack on the first round. You would lose to a singleton queen with West — yes — but you would pick up a singleton 9, 8, 7 or 4 in his hand. By retaining the king in dummy, you would be able to return for a second finesse against East's queen.

Now that you have the idea, test your skill on a full deal by covering the defenders' cards:

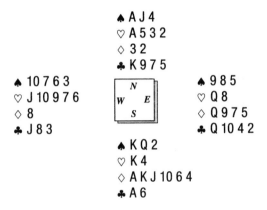

```
              ♠ A J 4
              ♡ A 5 3 2
              ◇ 3 2
              ♣ K 9 7 5
♠ 10 7 6 3        N        ♠ 9 8 5
♡ J 10 9 7 6              ♡ Q 8
◇ 8         W       E     ◇ Q 9 7 5
♣ J 8 3           S       ♣ Q 10 4 2
              ♠ K Q 2
              ♡ K 4
              ◇ A K J 10 6 4
              ♣ A 6
```

How would you play 7NT when West leads the ♡J?

You can count seven top tricks in the other three suits, so you need six diamond tricks. With eight cards missing, you will finesse East for the queen, rather than playing for the drop. The only remaining question is: should you cash the ace before crossing to dummy to finesse the jack?

No, you shouldn't. As before, cashing the ace would pick up a singleton queen with West. It would lead to defeat, however, when West holds a singleton spot-card, which is four times more likely. By cashing the ace first, you would permit yourself only one finesse in the suit. You would not be able to pick up queen fourth with East.

Secondary finesses

Some finesses are simply 50% shots — they either win or they lose. Look at this suit:

```
                    ♡ K Q 5
                 ┌─────────┐
                 │    N    │
   ♡ ???         │ W     E │        ♡ ???
                 │    S    │
                 └─────────┘
                    ♡ 4 3 2
```

You can always make one heart trick, but by leading twice towards dummy's honors you give yourself a 50-50 chance of a second trick in the suit. When West holds the ace you can score two heart tricks; when East has it you will be restricted to just one winner.

Let's make dummy's hearts slightly better:

```
                    ♡ K Q 10
                 ┌─────────┐
                 │    N    │
   ♡ ???         │ W     E │        ♡ ???
                 │    S    │
                 └─────────┘
                    ♡ 4 3 2
```

You lead a heart to the king and let's suppose first that the king loses to East's ace. You still have a chance of a second trick; you can finesse the ten on the second round. For this reason, it would be good defense for East to hold up his ace when holding something like A-x-x or A-x-x-x. When you led towards the Q-10 on the next round, you would then have a guess to make. Playing the queen would be right if West held the ace; playing the ten would be right if West held the jack and East the ace. Unless East gave away the position of the ace, by hesitating on the first round, you should generally play the queen on the second round. That's because many Easts will (incorrectly) win the first round when they hold the ace.

The ruffing finesse

We have already seen the type of finesse where you lead the queen from Q-J-10-x. The ace waits in dummy and will fall like an axe if West produces the king. In a trump contract the same effect can be achieved when you have a void acting as your axe. If the defender covers with the missing honor, you can ruff. Here is a typical deal involving the technique known as the 'ruffing finesse':

```
              ♠ Q 9 4 3
              ♡ A J 10 5
              ◊ 3 2
              ♣ A 8 3
♠ 7 6        ┌─────────┐      ♠ 8 5
♡ 2          │    N    │      ♡ K Q 8 7 6 3
◊ Q 10 8 6 4 │ W     E │      ◊ K J 7
♣ Q J 10 7 2 │    S    │      ♣ K 5
             └─────────┘
              ♠ A K J 10 2
              ♡ 9 4
              ◊ A 9 5
              ♣ 9 6 4
```

You play in four spades after East has opened the bidding with 1♡.
West leads the ♡2, an obvious singleton, and you win with dummy's
ace to avoid an adverse ruff. After drawing trumps in two rounds, you
pass the ♡9 to East's queen. Whatever East returns, you will be able to
cross to dummy and lead the ♡J. If East covers, you can ruff and return
to dummy to discard one of your losing clubs on the ♡10. If he fails to
cover, you will discard a club immediately. In either case an eventual
diamond ruff will bring your total to ten tricks.

It may seem that a club lead would make life more difficult, setting
up the defenders' winners in the suit before you have the chance to
establish a heart winner. You can still succeed on this particular layout
if you duck the first round of clubs. Since East started with only two
clubs, this will break the communications between the defenders.

Key points

1. When you hold an ace-queen combination and can afford a loser in the suit, it may be right to cash the ace first before leading towards the queen. This is particularly important when the opponents do not hold many cards in the suit and the chance of a singleton king is therefore greater.

2. When you do not have all of the intermediate cards, be wary of leading a high card towards a finesse. Prefer to lead low towards your major tenace, if the entry position will allow this. When unsure whether to lead a high card to a finesse, ask yourself: can I afford a cover?

3. A lack of entries may force you to lead a high card for a finesse, when you must retain the lead in the hand opposite the tenace in order to repeat the finesse.

4. With holdings such as Q-J-6-3 opposite A-7-5-2, there is generally little point in leading the queen. You are certain to lose one trick in the suit. By leading the queen, you will lose two tricks whenever the suit breaks 4-1. Instead, you should cash the ace and lead twice towards the Q-J. You can then succeed against a 4-1 break when the defender sitting over the ace holds the four-card length (or when the king is singleton).

QUIZ

A.

♣ Q 7 6

♣ ? ? ?

```
  N
W   E
  S
```

♣ ? ? ?

cowell al
4 ✓/

♣ A J 10 4 2

Which club should you lead from dummy if:
- (i) you have no outside entry to dummy?
- (ii) you have plenty of outside entries? ➝ *low club*

B.

♥ A J 4 2

♥ ? ? ?

```
  N
W   E
  S
```

♥ ? ? ?

not K
w 8 cds

♥ K 9 5 3

How should you play this suit if you need four heart tricks?

C.

♦ Q 10 9 4 3

♦ ? ? ?

```
  N
W   E
  S
```

♦ ? ? ?

♦ A 2

You cash the ♦A and then lead low towards dummy. No high cards have appeared. Needing four diamond tricks, do you play the queen or the ten from dummy?

not J

D.

♠ J 8 3 2

♠ ? ? ?

```
  N
W   E
  S
```

♠ ? ? ?

♠ A Q 9 7 6

What is your best play for five spade tricks, assuming you have adequate entries to both hands?

Answers

A. i) With no outside entry, you must start with the queen, aiming to retain the lead in dummy if the finesse wins. You can then repeat the finesse and score five club tricks whenever the suit divides 3-2 and East holds the king. If East started with a singleton king, you will lose a club trick; this is much less likely than East holding king third, in which case the queen lead is necessary.

ii) With outside entries, it is not important that you win the first round of clubs in dummy. You should therefore lead a low club in case East began with the singleton king.

B. Start by leading low to the jack. If the suit divides 3-2 either way, with West holding the queen, you will score four heart tricks. It does not help you to start with the king intending to finesse the jack on the second round. If East began with the singleton queen, you can never score four heart tricks, as West's ♡ 10-8-7-6 will always be a stopper.

Indeed, cashing the king first actually reduces your chances of four tricks, since it may be West who holds the singleton queen. In that case, leading low towards dummy on the first round of the suit enables you to take a third round finesse against East's remaining ♡ 10-8.

C. Play the queen. This will win whenever West began with ◇ K-x-x. Of course, playing the ten would win had West begun with ◇ J-x-x, so perhaps you think it is an even-money guess. However, there is a second way to win by playing the queen — East may have begun with a doubleton jack. You will then be able to force out West's king with your ten-nine to establish the long card in the suit.

It does not help to play the ten and force a doubleton king from East, as you will still have to lose a trick to West's remaining ◇ J-x.

D. It would be a mistake to lead the jack on the first round. If East held a singleton king you would lose a trick on the third round to West's ♠ 10-5-4. Instead you should play low to the queen. If only low cards appear from the defenders on this trick, you will play the ace next, hoping that the suit divides 2-2. If instead West produces the ten on the first round, you will return to dummy, in some other suit, to lead the jack through East's remaining ♠ K-x.

The Double Finesse

So far, we have concentrated on situations in which you were finessing against only one honor. You may have taken the same finesse more than once, but that was still only a single finesse.

In the next layout, you must finesse against two honors:

```
                    ◇ A J 10
                   ┌─────────┐
                   │    N    │
    ◇ ???          │ W     E │        ◇ ???
                   │    S    │
                   └─────────┘
                    ◇ 7 5 2
```

The objective is to score two diamond tricks and, assuming adequate entries to both hands, this can be done roughly three-quarters of the time — whenever West holds at least one of the missing honors.

You start by leading a diamond towards dummy, intending to finesse by playing the jack (or ten). If West holds both missing honors, it makes no difference whether he plays an honor or not. If he does, you will win with the ace and knock out his second honor with the J-10. If he plays low, your initial finesse will win.

Suppose now that the two missing honors are split. Your first finesse will lose to East's honor. When you regain the lead you will finesse again, scoring two tricks. You will be restricted to one trick only when East holds both missing honors.

Taking two finesses was possible here because all of the honors were in the same hand. Notice the difference in this next combination:

$\diamond$ A 10 3

$\diamond$???

$\boxed{\begin{matrix} & N & \\ W & & E \\ & S & \end{matrix}}$

$\diamond$???

$\diamond$ J 7 2

Your chances of scoring two diamond tricks are drastically reduced. Again you start with a low card to the ten. You will score two tricks when West holds both honors (which will happen roughly one quarter of the time), also on the rare occasions when he began with a singleton or a doubleton honor. When West holds one of the honors and it is guarded more than once, you cannot pick it up. It is no good leading the jack on the first round, of course, because West would cover. Indeed, playing in this fashion would cost you the second diamond trick when West holds honor doubleton.

Possession of the nine of diamonds (in either hand) would allow you to take two legitimate finesses, restoring your chances to the original 75%.

Assuming adequate intermediates, the mathematics of the double finesse apply irrespective of how many cards you hold in the suit. Whether the defenders hold eight cards or only four does not greatly alter the odds of West holding at least one of the missing honors. Even so, our next topic outlines a concept that some players simply refuse to believe...

The Principle of Restricted Choice

The Principle of Restricted Choice essentially says that you should assume a defender played a particular card because he was forced to do so, rather than because he chose to play it from two cards of equal value. With that idea in mind, how would you play this suit for no loser?

$\spadesuit$ A 10 7 6 5 4

$\spadesuit$???

$\boxed{\begin{matrix} & N & \\ W & & E \\ & S & \end{matrix}}$

$\spadesuit$???

$\spadesuit$ K 3 2

If you cash the king and only the two small spades appear from the defenders, you will need a 2-2 break. What if East follows with one of the honors, though? Should you play to the ace next or take a finesse?

The odds on each of the various defensive holdings are about the same. So, the probability that East started with a singleton jack, a singleton queen, or queen-jack doubleton are all roughly equal. If East follows with an honor when you cash the king, the odds are therefore 2:1 in favor of finessing.

That seems fairly straightforward. 'Ah, but wait a minute,' you may be thinking. 'Once I've cashed the king and he has followed with, say, the jack, the singleton queen disappears from the equation. The odds that he began with the singleton jack or the queen-jack doubleton are the same, so it's a 50-50 guess, isn't it?'

This is where the 'Restricted Choice' concept comes in. In itself, the odds of the singleton jack and the queen-jack doubleton are the same. However, when East is dealt the singleton jack he has no choice but to play it when the king is cashed. When he is dealt the queen-jack doubleton, though, he will play the queen some of the time and the jack some of the time. If we assume that he will play each honor about half of the time (although exactly how often he chooses each one will depend on the individual defender), then the odds are still 2-to-1 that he has played the jack because he had no choice.

Look at it this way. The thirty times that an honor appears from East can be broken down like this:

10 times he was dealt the queen and had to play it
10 times he was dealt the jack and had to play it
5 times he was dealt the QJ and chose to play the queen
5 times he was dealt the QJ and chose to play the jack

So, 10 times out of every 15 that the queen appears, the card was a singleton. The same applies when the jack appears. The Theory of Restricted Choice is entirely sound — believe us! You will meet players who will dispute it endlessly through the night. (We even know of one New Zealand international in this category!) Be happy to have the odds 2-to-1 in your favor when you play against them.

If we now add a few small cards to the suit combination we saw earlier, we can see that Restricted Choice is equally valid here:

◇ A J 10 9 8

◇ ???
| N |
| W   E |
| S |

◇ ???

◇ 7 6 5 4

You hold nine diamonds and your objective is to score four tricks in the suit. There are numerous ways to attempt this and each of them will win some of the time.

The three alternatives are (i) to cash the ace first, (ii) to take a finesse and, if it loses, to play the ace on the second round, and (iii) to take two finesses. Which do you think offers the best chance?

With so few possible distributions of the cards, it is fairly easy to see which option will work most often. If East holds ◊K-Q-x-(x) then no line of play works. If West holds either a singleton honor or ◊K-Q doubleton, then all options work. We will therefore ignore those cases. The odds of each of the possible defensive holdings are roughly equal, so let's try to discover the best line of play by counting the number of relevant holdings to which each line of play loses.

Cashing the ace first wins if East holds a singleton honor or the suit divides 2-2. It loses any time East holds one of the two low singletons or if he is void. That's three of the relevant cases.

Taking a first round finesse and, if it loses, cashing the ace next, wins if West holds both honors but it loses to the two cases when East starts with a singleton honor. Still, that's an improvement since it loses to only two of the key defensive holdings.

What about taking two finesses? To how many of the relevant defensive holdings does this lose? Right, just one — when East holds precisely ◊K-Q doubleton.

East was twice as likely to have started with a singleton honor as he was to hold precisely king-queen doubleton — the same 2:1 odds we saw earlier. Those odds have not changed because you have taken a losing finesse on the first round of the suit.

Before leaving the straightforward double finesse, let's look at a full deal on which you can apply the concepts outlined above. Cover the defenders' hands and decide how you would play.

```
              ♠ A K 4
              ♡ A 10 9 4
              ◇ 8 6 2
              ♣ 9 3 2
♠ 10 9 8 2      ┌──────┐      ♠ 7 6 3
♡ Q 8 7 6      │   N  │      ♡ J 5
◇ Q J 10 9     │ W  E │      ◇ K 7
♣ J            │   S  │      ♣ Q 10 8 7 6 4
               └──────┘
              ♠ Q J 5
              ♡ K 3 2
              ◇ A 5 4 3
              ♣ A K 5
```

You open with a strong 1NT. Your partner raises to game and West leads the ◇Q. East overtakes with the king, which you duck, and returns the diamond seven to West's nine. You take the third round of diamonds with the ace as East sheds a club.

You can count eight top tricks, and the chances of developing a ninth via a 3-3 diamond break have already dissolved. It seems that you need to score three heart tricks. How should you go about that?

One possibility is to cash both top honors hoping to drop a doubleton honor or to find the suit breaking 3-3. As it happens, that line of play will work on this deal, but it is a distinctly inferior option. It is easy to see why: not only will it lose on the six layouts where East holds a small doubleton heart, but also in those four cases where he began with a low singleton. That is ten of the possible defensive holdings. (West would have led a five-card heart suit, you may think, but with a solid diamond sequence this is not completely certain.)

A second alternative is to cash the king and then play to the ten on the second round. If the finesse loses to the jack or the queen, you could then play the ace on the third round, losing only to the eight cases where East began with a doubleton honor. Although that option fails miserably on this deal, it is still a slight improvement. However, you can double those odds by following Restricted Choice.

The best line of play is to cash the king of hearts and then to take two finesses. Lead low to the ten on the second round and, assuming your first finesse loses to the jack or the queen, take a second finesse on the third round. This loses only to four of the layouts where success is possible — when East began with precisely ♡Q-J-x. Do you see why Restricted Choice is relevant? Because when East wins the first finesse with the jack, say, it is more likely that he did so because he had to (it was his only honor) than that he chose to win with the jack when holding both honors. Once again, the double finesse, the line of play indicated by Restricted Choice, is a 2-to-1 favorite.

Other double finesses

This is another common finessing position:

```
              ♣ A Q 10
              ┌─────┐
              │  N  │
  ♣ ???       │ W  E│        ♣ ???
              │  S  │
              └─────┘
              ♣ 7 5 3
```

Seeking three club tricks you must find West with both the king and the jack. <u>Note that it is important to finesse the ten first.</u> You then return to the South hand and finesse the queen. If instead you finesse the queen first, you will have a definite loser in the suit, even when the queen wins. This position is similar:

```
              ♡ K J 5
              ┌─────┐
              │  N  │
  ♡ ???       │ W  E│        ♡ ???
              │  S  │
              └─────┘
              ♡ 6 4 3
```

Whether you make two, one, or no tricks, will depend on the position of the ace and queen. Again you must finesse the lower card first. Play to the jack on the first round, rather than to the king.

This is a little more complicated:

```
              ◇ A Q 9
              ┌─────┐
              │  N  │
  ◇ ???       │ W  E│        ◇ ???
              │  S  │
              └─────┘
              ◇ 6 3 2
```

How would you play to make two tricks?

If you finesse the queen on the first round, you will succeed only around 50% of the time. By leading low to the nine on the first round, you will succeed also when West holds both the jack and the ten. If he chooses not to insert an honor, the nine will force East's king. If instead he plays an honor, this will be covered by the queen and king and you can take a successful finesse of the nine on the second round. This increases the chance of two tricks to around 62%.

This position is similar:

```
              ♠ A J 9
                  N
  ♠ ? ? ?     W       E     ♠ ? ? ?
                  S
              ♠ 6 3 2
```

How would you play to make two tricks?

One option is to lead low to the jack, hoping to find West with both the king and the queen — roughly a 25% chance. Play to the nine on the first round and you will score two tricks when West holds the king and ten, or the queen and ten. This increases your chance of success to over 37%.

Your task with the next holding is to make only one trick:

```
              ◇ K 10 9                  9 then 10
                  N
  ◇ ? ? ?     W       E     ◇ ? ? ?
                  S
              ◇ 4 3 2
```

Start by leading low to the nine. This will bring immediate gratification if West started life with both the queen and the jack.

If the nine loses to the jack or the queen, it may seem that you have a guess on the second round. Should you play West for the missing middle honor or the ace? Think back to our discussion of Restricted Choice. The same reasoning applies here — the odds are 2:1 in favor of playing the ten on the second round. If East won the first round of diamonds with the jack, say, it is right to assume that he did so because he had no choice. (The same if he won with the queen, of course!)

The intra-finesse

The intra-finesse was discovered by Brazilian expert, Gabriel Chagas. Its purpose is to provide you with an alternative finesse when the bidding or some other indication suggests that a simple finesse will fail.

On the layout below, East has opened the bidding in hearts and thus you can be fairly sure that he has both the king and length in the suit. If West had been kind enough to lead his partner's suit, you would have

had no problem, but he struck out in some other direction. Can you see
how to make two heart tricks if you must attack the suit yourself?

$\heartsuit$ Q 8 2

$\heartsuit$ 10 5

	N	
W		E
	S	

$\heartsuit$ K J 7 6 4

$\heartsuit$ A 9 3

A simple finesse (leading towards the queen) will not help. Nor
will leading low from dummy intending to put in the nine.

The answer is to adopt the two-step strategy that is known as an
intra-finesse. Begin by leading a low heart from your hand. Assuming
that West plays the five, you put in dummy's eight, which loses to the
jack.

When you regain the lead, you can then lead the queen of hearts
from dummy, pinning West's ten and effectively finessing against East's
king at the same time.

Key points

1. It is still possible to finesse even if you are missing more than one
honor. With such as A-Q-10-x opposite x-x-x, finesse the ten on the
first round.

2. The Principle of Restricted Choice suggests that you should assume
a defender has played a particular card because he was forced to do
so, rather than because he chose to play it from equals.

3. When you suspect from the bidding or other information that the
simple finesse is destined to fail, consider an alternative such as the
intra-finesse.

C A. lead to 10, then to Q   CH. lead to 10
NO B. take A, lead to Q   tam K
X C. take A lead to 10
e D. lead Q
e E. finese 9
C F. not 9
  G. lead to 9, finse cash AK

In these quiz questions, you will meet some suit combinations that we have not discussed, but the answers can be worked out by applying the principles we have covered during the chapter. In each case, there are no clues from the bidding, or early play, to suggest that either defender is more likely to hold either the missing high cards or length in the suit.

A.

♣ 7 5 2

```
        N
   W         E
        S
```

♣ ? ? ?   ♣ ? ? ?

♣ Q 10 5

How can you give yourself the best chance of scoring a club trick?

B.

♡ Q 10 4 2

```
        N
   W         E
        S
```

♡ ? ? ?   ♡ ? ? ?

♡ A 7 5 3

How should you play to bring in the heart suit for only one loser?

C.

◇ A 7

```
        N
   W         E
        S
```

◇ ? ? ?   ◇ ? ? ?   *surprise*

◇ Q 10 9 8 6

How should you play to score four diamond tricks?

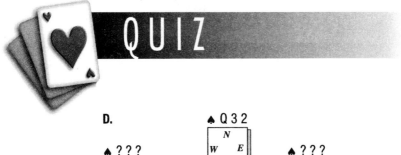

D.

♠ Q 3 2

	N	
W		E
	S	

♠ ? ? ?

♠ ? ? ?

♠ A 10 9 8

What line of play gives you the best chance of scoring three spade tricks?

E.

♠ Q 9 7 5

	N	
W		E
	S	

♠ ? ? ?

♠ ? ? ?

♠ A K 4

You need to score four spade tricks. When you play the ace and king, East drops the ten on the second round. You lead a third round and the eight appears from West. Should you finesse the nine now or rise with the queen?

F.

♡ A K 9 7 5 2

	N	
W		E
	S	

♡ ? ? ?

♡ ? ? ?

♡ Q 4

You need to score six heart tricks. You start by cashing the queen, on which East drops the ten. West follows with a low card on the second round. Should you now finesse the nine or cash the ace and the king?

G.

$\diamond$? ? ?
　　　　$\diamond$ A 10 5 2
　　　　N
　　　W　E
　　　　S
　　　　$\diamond$ K 9 3
　　　　　　　$\diamond$? ? ?

How will you play to score three diamond tricks?

H.

$\clubsuit$? ? ?
　　　　$\clubsuit$ K 10 5 2
　　　　N
　　　W　E
　　　　S
　　　　$\clubsuit$ 7 6 4 3
　　　　　　　$\clubsuit$? ? ?

How will you play to score two club tricks?

Answers

A. There are two possibilities — to lead to the queen (playing East for A-K), or to lead to the ten (playing East for K-J or A-J). Clearly it is better to succeed in two situations rather than just one, so you should play low to the ten on the first round.

B. You should cash the ace on the first round, guarding against a singleton honor with East. When you then lead a second round towards dummy, the nine appears on the left. Should you play the queen or the ten from dummy? When the suit breaks 3-2, it is an open guess — the queen will work well if East's remaining card is the jack, the ten will succeed if East's last card is the king. However, it is a better prospect, in the long run, to finesse dummy's ten because this will succeed also against K-J-9-x with West.

C. This is one of those combinations where you can work out the best line by counting how many of the possible defensive holdings each option loses to. There is no winning option if a defender holds ◇K-J-x-x-(x), so we can discount that one.

What are the possibilities? We could start by cashing the ace and then leading towards the ten. This will lose if West began with ◇K-J-x (four holdings) or with ◇J-x (four holdings). It will also lose also when either defender holds ◇K-x, since we will still have to lose a trick to the jack. That's eight more for a total of sixteen losing holdings. Not a good start!

How about cashing the ace and leading up to the queen? This is significantly better, as it wins against ◇J-x with West. We are left with just twelve losing holdings.

Finally, let's try leading the queen from your hand. This will lose if East has ◇K-J-x (four holdings) and if East holds ◇K-x (four), but that is all, since it not only picks up ◇J-x in either hand but also ◇K-x with West. A surprising winner, don't you think?

D. This time you have both adequate intermediates and sufficient length in the short hand to repeat the finesse as often as you need. Start by leading the queen and running it if East does not cover.

If the queen wins, you should next lead low to the nine (guarding against East holding both the king and the jack). If the nine loses to the jack, you can return to dummy in a side suit to take a third-round finesse against East's presumed king.

If the queen loses to West's king on the first round, you can still take and repeat a second finesse, bringing home three spade tricks whenever East started with at least one of the missing honors.

E. This is a Restricted Choice position. East is more likely to have played the ten on the second round because he had to (it was his last card) than because he chose it from two equal cards (jack and ten). The odds are roughly 2-to-1 in favor of finessing the nine on the third round.

F. Is this a Restricted Choice position? If you could be certain that East's ten was either a singleton or a chosen card from J-10, Restricted Choice would indeed apply. You would be justified in finessing the nine on the second round. There is another possibility, though: East's ten might be a mischievous false card from J-10-x, encouraging you to finesse when the suit is splitting 3-2 all along. If you judge that East is good enough to make such a false card, you should play for the drop.

G. The best first move is to finesse the nine. This will allow you to score three tricks when East started with a doubleton honor. Suppose the first finesse loses, to the queen or jack, and only small cards appear when you subsequently cash the king. The best chance on the third round is to rise with dummy's ace.

H. If your first move is a club to the king, you will score two tricks only when the ace is onside (and the suit breaks 3-2). A better idea it to lead to the ten on the first round. You will then score two tricks when West started with Q-J-x. If the ten loses to a middle honor, you will lead towards the king on the second round.

Which Finesse... And When?

So far we have concentrated on the mechanics of finessing in a single suit. Mastery of these techniques alone will sometimes be enough to bring home your contract. More often, though, you will have a choice of suits to attack, some of which will involve finesse positions.

Should you take a finesse or rely on some other chance? How should you decide which finesse to take? And at what point in the hand should you take it? Perhaps you intend to take more than one finesse — in which order should you take them?

Indeed, there will also be deals on which you should refuse to take any of the available finesses. Let's look at some examples to see how you can answer these questions.

Combining finesse and break chances

Assuming there are no other factors to influence matters, the odds on a simple finesse are a straight 50-50. If your contract relies on nothing more than taking a winning finesse, half the time you will register a plus and half the time you will go down. You will be successful more often if you combine chances in more than one suit.

A suit divides 3-3 little more than one third of the time. If you are forced to rely on either a 3-3 break or a finesse, you would therefore choose the finesse. Things are often not that simple, though. How would you tackle this contract?

```
              ♠ K Q 10 2
              ♡ 9 6 3
              ◇ A J 3
              ♣ 8 3 2
                  ┌─────┐
 ♡Q led           │  N  │
                  │W   E│
                  │  S  │
                  └─────┘
              ♠ A J 9 4
              ♡ 7 4              4S
              ◇ K 4 2
              ♣ A K 5 4
```

You play in four spades and the defense opens with three rounds of hearts. You ruff the third round and draw trumps in three rounds. You have nine tricks — five spades, including the heart ruff, plus the two minor-suit ace-kings. You can score a tenth trick via a successful diamond finesse (50%) or by finding the clubs 3-3 (36%). On which of these chances should you rely?

The answers to the question are neither and both. You do not have to choose between the two — you can combine the chances. How should you go about this?

Let's see what happens if you first take the better of the two chances — the diamond finesse. Suppose it loses. Can you then take advantage of a 3-3 club break? No, since you must give up a club before you can score the long trick in the suit. Having already lost three tricks — two hearts and one diamond — you cannot now afford to lose a club trick too.

Here is a general rule that can be applied to most situations in which you combine chances in more than one suit: start by playing on the suit in which you must lose a trick even if the suit behaves as you need it to.

Here, that suit is clubs — you must lose a trick in the suit before you can benefit from a 3-3 break. Let's see how the hand should be played: ruff the third round of hearts and draw trumps (we will assume that they break 3-2). You then play a low club from both hands. When you regain the lead, test the clubs. If they break 3-3, you are home. If they don't, you can still take the diamond finesse. In this way, you improve your chances to 68% — significantly better than either of the individual chances in isolation.

Why settle for one finesse when you can take two?

On the last deal you combined the chance of a break in one suit with a finesse in another. In the same way you can sometimes combine the chance of two finesses. How would you play this hand?

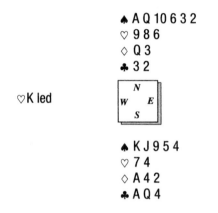

♠ A Q 10 6 3 2
♡ 9 8 6
◇ Q 3
♣ 3 2

♡K led

♠ K J 9 5 4
♡ 7 4
◇ A 4 2
♣ A Q 4

low D

You arrive in four spades, against silent opponents. West attacks with the king and queen of hearts and then leads a third heart to his partner's ace. How would you play?

You have two hearts and one diamond to lose. The contract therefore hinges on the club finesse... Or does it?

In fact, you have a choice of finesses: you can take a straightforward finesse against East for the king of clubs or you can lead a diamond towards dummy's queen, thereby finessing West for the diamond king. Which of these finesses should you take?

The answer is that you can take them both provided you do so in the right order. Which should you take first? This is easily worked out by applying the rule we met earlier: start by playing on the suit in which you must lose a trick even if the suit behaves as you need it to.

If you take the club finesse and it loses, will you then be able to take advantage of West holding the king of diamonds? No, because by the time you lead a diamond towards the queen you will already have lost two hearts and club. The king of diamonds will be the setting trick.

The correct play is to ruff the third heart, draw trumps ending in the South hand, and then lead a low diamond towards the queen.

If West holds the king of diamonds, he can take the third defensive trick with it. You will then have ten tricks: six trump tricks in dummy, one ruff in hand, two diamonds and one club. The position of the king of clubs is irrelevant.

If instead the queen of diamonds had lost to the king, you would still be able to fall back on the club finesse for your tenth trick. By taking the diamond finesse first, you are able to combine your chances.

This concept appears in many guises. How would you play to combine your chances on this deal?

♠ K 8
♡ K Q 9 8 6 4
◊ 5 3 2
♣ 8 4

```
      N
   W     E
      S
```

♠7 led

♠ A Q J 3
♡ A 10 7 3 2
◊ K 6
♣ A Q

dump 2/D½

How do you play a contract of six hearts on a spade lead?

There are eleven top tricks — six hearts, four spades and the ace of clubs — and you have a choice of minor-suit finesses for the twelfth. So, should you play East for the king of clubs or the ace of diamonds?

It seems that you must choose one or the other. After all, if you take the club finesse and it loses, the defenders can cash the ace of diamonds to defeat you. Alternatively, playing a diamond to the king may be equally fatal if West holds the ace. He will then be able to cash a second diamond trick before you can try the club finesse.

The rule mentioned earlier should tell you which finesse to attempt first — the one in the suit where even a winning finesse will enable the defenders to score a trick, so diamonds here. Before taking the diamond finesse, though, you must take precautions against it losing. Win the opening lead in dummy, draw trumps, and cash your spade winners, discarding two diamonds from dummy. You can then safely enter dummy in trumps and lead a diamond towards the king.

If the ace of diamonds is onside, you will score your twelfth trick in diamonds. If instead the diamond finesse loses, you will still be able to take the club finesse for your contract.

The concept of combining your chances is a vital one, so here is one final example of the principle. If you feel like a mental workout, cover the defenders' cards and take over from declarer:

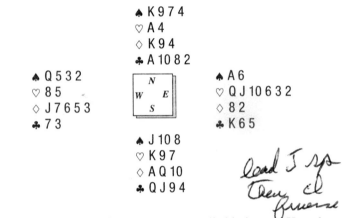

You declare 3NT after East has overcalled in hearts. How do you play when West leads the ♡8?

There are six top tricks — three diamonds, two hearts and one club. Finding West with the club king would quickly elevate that tally to nine, but what if the club finesse is wrong? With East favorite to hold the ace of spades, that would be the end of your chances.

Is there any rush to take the club finesse? No — if the club king is onside, you can always fall back on that finesse later. Instead, you should first try to take advantage of your second 50-50 chance — finding the queen of spades onside.

You should duck the first round of hearts and win the heart continuation with dummy's ace. Cross to the South hand in diamonds and lead the ♠J, intending to run it if West does not cover.

If the cards lie as shown in the diagram, you will be able to drive out East's ace of spades and later repeat the finesse against West's queen to score three tricks in that suit. You will then have nine tricks without even taking the club finesse.

If the first round of spades loses to East's queen, you abandon that suit and turn to clubs, combining your chances in the two black suits. If you begin with the club finesse, you will be unable to take advantage of the favorable spade position.

Choosing which finesse to take

Sometimes the entry position allows you to take only one of two finesses. How should you choose which? This is the type of situation we have in mind:

```
              ♠ K 7 2
              ♡ 6 3 2
              ♢ 8 6 3
              ♣ K Q 3 2
                  ┌─────┐
  ♣J led          │  N  │
                  │ W E │
                  │  S  │
                  └─────┘
              ♠ A 6 4
              ♡ A Q J 10 9
              ♢ A Q J
              ♣ 5 4
```

try D first

West leads the ♣J against four hearts. When you cover with the king, East wins with the ace and returns a club. What now?

You have a certain loser in spades and must therefore avoid a loser in one of the red suits. The spade king represents the only further entry to dummy, so you will be able to take just two finesses. Should you play a trump to the queen next, or a diamond to the queen?

The general plan will be to take one of the finesses and, if it succeeds, to use the ♠K to repeat that same finesse. If instead the first finesse loses, you will need a solitary finesse in the other red suit to pick up the suit.

Suppose you start with trump finesse. If this finesse succeeds, you will cross in spades and repeat it. Even if East does hold the trump king, you will still lose a trump trick when he holds four trumps. For this reason it is better to finesse in diamonds. When the king is onside, you know that a second finesse will save you a loser in that suit.

A second advantage of playing on diamonds comes when you

consider the case of the first finesse losing. If the diamond finesse fails, you still have a reasonably healthy chance of finding East with K-x of trumps (when one finesse will be good enough to pick up the suit). If you start with a losing trump finesse, there is much less chance of finding East with K-x of diamonds. That's because there are seven diamonds missing and only five hearts.

Key points

1. You can often combine chances in more than one suit. Sometimes this will mean testing a suit for an even break, falling back on a finesse elsewhere if the first suit does not lie favorably.

2. When combining chances in two different suits, the order in which you test those chances will often be crucial. As a general rule, you should play first on the suit where you will have to concede a trick even if the suit lies as you wish.

3. On some deals, you will be forced to choose between taking one finesse or another, perhaps because entries do not permit you to take both. Before deciding, ask yourself two questions: 'Will I make the contract if this finesse wins?' and 'Will I still have an alternative chance if this finesse loses?'

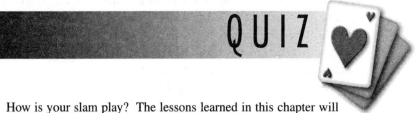

How is your slam play? The lessons learned in this chapter will help you bring home both of these contracts...

A.

```
        ♠ 8
        ♡ A K 5 4
        ◇ 6 5 4
        ♣ A J 7 4 2
♠K led
          N
        W   E
          S

        ♠ A 5 3
        ♡ J 7
        ◇ A Q 3
        ♣ K Q 10 8 3
```

good

You open 1♣ and West overcalls 1♠. West eventually leads the ♠K against your 6♣ contract. How do you play?

B.

```
        ♠ A Q
        ♡ Q 10 8 5 4
        ◇ A 8 4
        ♣ Q 9 2
♠3 led
          N
        W   E
          S

        ♠ 10 8 3
        ♡ A K J 7
        ◇ 7 3
        ♣ A J 10 3
```

good

West leads the ♠3 against your 6♡ contract. How do you play?

Answers

A. One simple line of play is to take the diamond finesse at some point. If it fails, though, you are likely to go down. There is a second finessing possibility in hearts, where you can lead towards the jack. If East holds the queen, you will make the slam whether or not he goes in with the queen. You can combine both of these finessing chances, provided you play on hearts before diamonds. You will be following the general rule of playing first on the suit where you will need to lose the lead even if the suit lies favorably. So, the best play (after drawing trumps) is to lead a low heart to the jack.

You may have spotted a second chance of making the contract. If West holds four hearts, you can draw trumps, ruff two spades and heart. You can then lead a fourth round of hearts from dummy, throwing one of your diamond losers. When West wins, he will have to lead a diamond into your tenace or concede a ruff-and-discard. However, after West's 1♠ overcall (cleverly introduced by the authors...) West is less likely to hold four hearts than East. Taking two finesses, as described above, is consequently the best shot.

B. Were you tempted to take the spade finesse? You shouldn't have been! If the spade finesse loses, you will go down for sure, since there is an unavoidable diamond loser to come. What is more, a successful spade finesse will not help you in the slightest. You will still need the club finesse to be right; otherwise you will lose a club and a diamond.

Since the spade finesse is a no-win proposition, you should rise with the spade ace. After drawing trumps, you can then take the club finesse. If this succeeds you will be able to throw the ♠Q from dummy, escaping for just one diamond loser.

The contract is a simple 50% proposition, depending solely on the club finesse. If you finesse the spade queen at Trick 1, you will succeed only 25% of the time, when both black-suit kings are onside.

CHAPTER • 4

The Two-Way Finesse

....

When you are missing the queen of a suit and can finesse either defender for it, this is known as a two-way finesse. Going down because you misguess a two-way finesse is always annoying. You cannot even claim you were unlucky, as you can when a straightforward finesse fails.

This is the most common two-way finesse position:

```
              ◇ A J 6
            ┌─────────┐
            │    N    │
  ◇ ? ? ?   │ W     E │   ◇ ? ? ?
            │    S    │
            └─────────┘
              ◇ K 10 3
```

Without any clues, it is a 50-50 guess whether you finesse the jack or the ten. In real life, you will rarely come across a blind guess. Perhaps East opened the bidding and the defenders hold only 14 points between them. He will then be a strong favorite to hold the queen.

On the following deal you can give yourself the best chance by obtaining a count on the defenders' hands:

....

```
                    ♠ A 10
                    ♡ A K Q 3
                    ◇ A J 10 7
                    ♣ A Q J
    ♠ Q 8 2         ┌──────────┐      ♠ J 7 5 3
    ♡ 8 5 4         │    N     │      ♡ 10 7 2
    ◇ 9 5 3         │ W     E  │      ◇ Q 8 6 4
    ♣ 10 9 8 3      │    S     │      ♣ 7 6
                    └──────────┘
                    ♠ K 9 6 4
                    ♡ J 9 6
                    ◇ K 2
                    ♣ K 5 4 2
```

You play in 7NT from the South hand and the ♣10 is led. You have twelve top tricks and success will depend on taking the two-way finesse in diamonds the right way. Rather than making this decision at an early stage, you should play your winners in hearts and clubs. This reveals that West holds seven cards in these suits, East only five. Since East therefore holds eight cards in spades and diamonds to West's six, he is more likely to hold the diamond queen. You run dummy's jack of diamonds through East and on this occasion the favorite comes romping home.

Even in the absence of any distributional information, it may still be better to finesse one way rather than another. Look at this suit:

```
                    ♡ A J 6 4
                    ┌──────────┐
    ♡ ? ? ?         │    N     │      ♡ ? ? ?
                    │ W     E  │
                    │    S     │
                    └──────────┘
                    ♡ K 10 3
```

You need four tricks from this heart suit.

If someone whispered in your ear that hearts were 3-3, you would be faced with a 50-50 guess. Suppose, instead, that a count revealed that one of the defenders began with a doubleton heart. As the odds favor the defender with the length to hold the queen by a 4:2 margin, you might think you should finesse against that defender. Before doing so, though, ask yourself whether a winning finesse will help you. Lacking the ♡9, you cannot make four heart tricks if either defender began with queen fourth. You should therefore play off the ace and king hoping to drop a doubleton queen. The odds may not be very good, but they are the best available in the circumstances.

This situation is slightly different:

```
              ♠ A J 6 5 2
                 ┌─────┐
                 │  N  │
   ♠ ? ? ?       │ W E │       ♠ ? ? ?
                 │  S  │
                 └─────┘
              ♠ K 10
```

If you knew that spades were 3-3, it would again be a 50-50 guess as to whether you should play West or East for queen third. If the suit divides 4-2, there is only one situation that will allow you to score five spade tricks — a doubleton queen in the East hand. You should therefore begin by playing a low spade to the ten on the first round.

Enlisting the defenders' help

Two-way finesse positions frequently feature in endplays, since the best way to avoid a guess is to force the opponents to lead the key suit. Let's go back to our original suit, the one where there was nothing to indicate who held the queen, and put it into a full deal.

Cover the defenders' cards and take declarer's seat:

```
                     ♠ 7 5
                     ♡ A Q 10 7 5 2
                     ◇ A J 6
                     ♣ K 4
   ♠ K 10 6 3          ┌─────┐        ♠ J 9 8 4 2
   ♡ 9                 │  N  │        ♡ 8
   ◇ 9 7 5 2           │ W E │        ◇ Q 8 4
   ♣ J 9 6 3           │  S  │        ♣ Q 10 8 2
                       └─────┘
                     ♠ A Q
                     ♡ K J 6 4 3
                     ◇ K 10 3
                     ♣ A 7 5
```

You reach an excellent small slam in hearts and West leads a trump. How would you play?

Your prospects are excellent. Having digested the chapters on combining your chances, your immediate impression may be that this contract has at least a 75% chance — you can try the spade finesse first and, if that fails, fall back on guessing which way to finesse in diamonds.

If that was how you analyzed the hand, look again! This time imagine that, instead of the spade queen, your second spade was a low one. You might then think of an endplay: win the opening lead, draw a second round of trumps, cash the top clubs, and ruff the third round in dummy to eliminate that suit. You then play ace and a second spade.

It matters not at all which defender wins this trick. He will have to a choice of losing options. If he returns a black suit, that will give you a ruff-and-discard, allowing you to dispose of your potential loser in diamonds. Alternatively, if he exits with a diamond, you will score three diamond tricks wherever the queen is.

The correct line of play is no different on the actual hand, where your second spade is the queen. The spade finesse is a red herring and the contract is 100% — draw trumps, eliminate the clubs, cash the ace of spades, and exit with the spade queen to endplay whichever defender holds the king.

Now that you have the idea, take a look at this suit:

```
              ♠ A 9 2
             ┌─────────┐
             │    N    │
 ♠ ???       │ W     E │      ♠ ???
             │    S    │
             └─────────┘
              ♠ K 10 3
```

At first glance, you do not appear to have a finesse to take here. You can, however, create a finessing position if you can force the defenders to lead the first round of spades. Suppose this is the full deal:

```
                  ♠ A 9 2
                  ♡ A 7 3
                  ◇ A 10 6
                  ♣ K J 8 3
    ♠ Q 8 4      ┌─────────┐     ♠ J 7 6 3
    ♡ J 9 2      │    N    │     ♡ Q 10 5 4
    ◇ 9 8 3 2    │ W     E │     ◇ Q J 7 5
    ♣ 6 5 2      │    S    │     ♣ 7
                 └─────────┘
                  ♠ K 10 5
                  ♡ K 8 6
                  ◇ K 4
                  ♣ A Q 10 9 4
```

West leads a trump against your contract of six clubs. You draw trumps in three rounds and eliminate the diamond suit. You then play three rounds of hearts, West winning the third round. He must now open the spade suit or concede a fatal ruff-and-discard.

Suppose first that he exits with the ♠4. You play low from dummy and capture East's jack with your king. A finesse in spades has now been established — low to dummy's ♠9 brings home the contract.

Perhaps West is a little more cunning. As he can see that the position is lost unless his partner holds either the king or jack of spades, he may choose to exit with the spade queen. What should you do now?

If West holds both honors, you need to win with the king and finesse the nine. If instead East holds the spade jack, you must win with the ace and finesse the ten.

Against competent defenders you can safely assume that the spade honors are divided, leaving East with the spade jack. Why is that? Because if West held ♠Q-J-x the defenders would have arranged for East to win the third round of hearts. A spade lead from his side would then give nothing away.

Here is another deal where you can force the defenders to assist you in your finessing:

```
                    ♠ A J 10
                    ♡ K J 6 4
                    ◇ K 6 4
                    ♣ A Q 3
     ♠ Q 8 6 5      ┌─────────┐      ♠ K 9 7 3 2
     ♡ 5            │ N       │      ♡ 9 8
     ◇ J 10 9 3     │ W   E   │      ◇ 8 7 2
     ♣ J 9 8 7      │ S       │      ♣ K 10 5
                    └─────────┘
                    ♠ 4
                    ♡ A Q 10 7 3 2
                    ◇ A Q 5
                    ♣ 6 4 2
```

West leads the ◇J against your small slam in hearts. How would you enlist the defenders' help?

You should win the diamond lead, draw trumps in two rounds, then play the two remaining diamond winners, ending in your hand. If you finesse the ♣Q now, the finesse will fail and you will go down. Instead you should play a spade to the jack. If West holds both missing spade honors you will score two spade tricks, whether or not he chooses to split his honors on the first round. If instead East holds one or more spade honors, he will win the first round and find himself endplayed. A diamond (if he still has one) will concede a ruff-and-discard. A return of either black suit will run into a tenace in the dummy, again giving you a twelfth trick.

The two-way ruffing finesse

A ruffing finesse can sometimes be two-way as well. Suppose you have the following side suit in a trump contract:

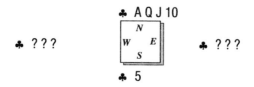

♣ ? ? ?   ♣ A Q J 10   ♣ ? ? ?

♣ 5

Suppose, first, that you have outside entries to dummy and plenty of trumps in your hand. If you need to score only two club tricks without losing the lead, you have a genuine guess. If West holds the king, you must take a straightforward finesse by leading from your hand and putting in one of dummy's lower honors. If East holds the club king, you must cross to the ace and lead the second round from dummy, discarding if East follows with a low card and ruffing out the king if he plays it. (You can increase your prospects marginally by ruffing the second round anyway, to catch an original doubleton king with West.)

Only by discovering that perhaps one defender holds five clubs to his partner's three, or by a count of the high-card points based on the bidding, can you improve your chances of guessing correctly.

More often, though, you will require three tricks from the club suit. That's easy enough if you can afford to lose a trick to the king first, but what if you cannot? In the absence of any external evidence, which way should you finesse then?

If you play East for the king, and he does prove to hold that card, you will always score three tricks from the suit. You will cash the ace and lead the remaining honors until the king appears, when you will ruff in the South hand. If instead you play West for the king, the position is nowhere near so rosy. You can take the finesse only once. Thereafter you will have to cash the ace and ruff a club. You will succeed only when West holds ♣K-x-x or ♣K-x. The ruffing finesse is therefore the better chance. It answers in the affirmative the question 'will I make my contract if this finesse wins?' The straightforward finesse does not.

Combining your chances to avoid a finesse

To conclude this chapter, let's look at a deal where you have two-way finesses in two different suits. In order to combine your options, giving yourself the best chance, you must decide which way to finesse, and in which suit. If page 51 in this book of ours does not find you too exhausted, cover the defenders' cards and take the South seat.

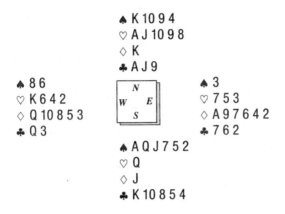

♠ K 10 9 4
♡ A J 10 9 8
◇ K
♣ A J 9

♠ 8 6   ♠ 3
♡ K 6 4 2   ♡ 7 5 3
◇ Q 10 8 5 3   ◇ A 9 7 6 4 2
♣ Q 3   ♣ 7 6 2

♠ A Q J 7 5 2
♡ Q
◇ J
♣ K 10 8 5 4

You arrive in six spades and West leads a diamond to his partner's ace, East returning a trump. You draw a second round of trumps, East discarding a diamond. What next?

There are nine top tricks — six trumps, the ace of hearts, and two top clubs. You have a conventional two-way finesse position in clubs and a two-way ruffing finesse in hearts. With a diamond trick already lost, you cannot afford to take a losing finesse. Should you try to establish three extra club tricks or three extra heart tricks?

For reasons we have already seen, a straightforward heart finesse against West will not establish enough winners (unless West started with K-x or K-x-x). It therefore seems that you must choose between taking the ruffing finesse in hearts and playing one or other defender for the queen of clubs.

This gives you a choice of three possible finesses, all of which rate to be approximately 50-50 shots. The problem is that each one is mutually exclusive — if you take a finesse and it loses, you are down right away without being able to try one of the others. Nevertheless, there is a way to combine two different chances. Can you see how?

The finesse you plan to take, as a last resort, is the ruffing heart finesse. Before committing yourself to this 50% chance, it cannot cost to cash the two top clubs. More than 30% of the time, the queen will come down singleton or doubleton, as it does in the diagram above.

Curiously, on a deal that offered you a choice of four different finesses, you actually took none.

More commonly you may need to combine your chances when you have a choice between two straightforward (non-ruffing) finesses. That's the case here:

♠ Q 6
♡ J 10 9 3
◇ K J 7 6
♣ K 7 2

♠ 4 led

```
      N
  W       E
      S
```

♠ J 7
♡ K Q 7 6 2
◇ A 4 3
♣ A J 5

You arrive in four hearts and the defenders cash two rounds of spades before switching to ace and another trump. The trumps break 2-2 and you must now seek the best chance in the minor suits. A failing finesse will be fatal, so you would like to play for the drop in one suit before falling back on a finesse in the second suit if necessary. Which minor suit offers the better chance of dropping the missing queen?

Right, diamonds — because you hold seven diamonds between the hands and only six clubs. If the diamond queen does not drop in two rounds you will finesse the ♣J.

Key points

1. When you are faced with a two-way finesse for a queen, try to discover which defender holds greater length in the suit. He will be a favorite to hold the missing honor.

2. Even when you have good reason to think a particular defender holds the missing queen, ensure that you can still make the contract if that is indeed the case. Do not be afraid to buck the percentages if doing so offers you the only chance for your contract. If you know that the suit is breaking 4-2 but cannot pick up Q-x-x-x, play for the queen to be doubleton.

3. When faced with the classic two-way guess for a queen, look for a way to force the defenders to open the suit.

4. When you have to choose between finesses to make the contract, it is often possible to combine two chances — playing for the drop in one suit, then falling back on a finesse in the other suit. Play for the drop in the suit where the defenders hold fewer cards.

A.

♠ A J 4
♡ A 4
◇ A 4
♣ A J 9 7 3 2

♡ Q led

```
    N
 W     E
    S
```

♠ K 10 5 3
♡ K
◇ K Q J 10 5 3
♣ K 10

West leads the queen of hearts against 7NT. When you cash the ace of diamonds, West discards a heart. How do you play?

B.

♠ A Q 4
♡ 6 5
◇ A Q J 10
♣ A 9 7 3

♣ K led

```
    N
 W     E
    S
```

♠ K 5
♡ K 8
◇ 4 3
♣ J 10 8 6 5 4 2

You are declarer in five clubs. West leads the ♣K and you win the ace, East throwing a heart. You have a choice of three finesses — a heart to the king, a straightforward diamond finesse, or a ruffing finesse in diamonds (having thrown a diamond from hand on the third round of spades). Which finesse do you take? Can you see a way to guarantee your contract?

Answers

A. When the diamonds prove to be 5-0, perhaps you conclude that West, who has thirteen non-diamonds to East's eight, is more likely to hold any specific card, notably the black queens. Indeed, this is a valid assumption, but it still only improves the odds on a black-suit finesse through West from 50-50 to 13-8 (or a little over 60%).

Rather than guessing which black-suit finesse to take, you should look for a way to combine your chances. You can do this by attempting to drop one black queen before taking a finesse against the queen in the other suit.

Which queen should you try to bring down doubleton? As there are six spades missing and only five clubs, it is more likely that the club queen will be only once guarded. If the queen of clubs does not come down, you would run your diamonds, play the king of spades, and finesse West for the spade queen.

B. On this deal, you have a choice of three finesses — a lead towards the king in hearts, a straightforward finesse of the diamond queen, or a ruffing finesse in diamonds. If you rely exclusively on any of these, your chances are just 50%. The correct line of play involves taking none of the finesses! You should play three rounds of spades, throwing a diamond from your hand. You then cash the ◊ A and exit with a trump to West's queen. What can he return? A spade will give a ruff-and-discard; a heart will set up your king; a diamond will be through the Q-J-10 up to your void. Eleven tricks, whatever West does.

CHAPTER 5

Defending Against the Finesse

When declarer takes a finesse, it is destined either to win or to fail. There is little you can do as a defender to change that. Or is there?

In itself, this is true, but as we have seen in our investigation of the subject from declarer's point of view, there is rather more than meets the eye when it comes to finessing. The same is true when you are defending against a finesse. There are numerous weapons available for the defenders and the most important of these is the hold-up.

Encouraging declarer to repeat a losing finesse

Take the East cards on this next deal and see what you make of the situation:

```
                 ♠ 7 2
                 ♡ A Q 2
                 ◇ A 6 3
                 ♣ A Q J 10 6
 ♠ Q J 10 8 5    ┌─────────┐   ♠ 9 6 4
 ♡ K 10 8 4      │   N     │   ♡ J 6 3
 ◇ K 5           │ W   E   │   ◇ Q J 10 7
 ♣ 9 3           │   S     │   ♣ K 8 4
                 └─────────┘
                 ♠ A K 3
                 ♡ 9 7 5
                 ◇ 9 8 4 2
                 ♣ 7 5 2
```

WEST	NORTH	EAST	SOUTH
	1♣	pass	1NT
pass	2NT	pass	3NT
all pass			

You partner leads the ♠Q and declarer wins with the ace. His next move is a club to dummy's queen. How will you defend?

What will happen if you take the first round of clubs with the king? It is not hard to predict. Declarer will win the spade return and take his only remaining chance — the heart finesse. When it succeeds, he will have nine tricks.

Now try something different. When declarer plays a club to the queen, follow smoothly with a low card. Things are not so easy for declarer now, are they? He has only one entry back to his hand and must guess whether to finesse in hearts or to repeat the club finesse. If he concludes from your duck that the club king is onside, he may well decide to use that entry to play on clubs. It's true that he will also need a 3-2 break in the suit, but this is a better chance than the heart finesse (if the club king is indeed onside). In any case it is better to give the declarer some sort of losing option than none at all. A skilled defender might well hold up even when holding king doubleton.

The diamond suit below represents a similar situation. Declarer is playing in notrump and has no side entry to a dummy that contains this precious asset:

◇ A K J 10 3

◇ ???

```
  N
W   E
  S
```

◇ ???

◇ 7 4

When declarer leads the first round of diamonds to the ten, his life is made much easier if the finesse loses. He can then count on four diamond tricks unless the suit happens to split 5-1.

Against experienced defenders, though, his first finesse is virtually guaranteed to win. Indeed, sitting East, you should duck smoothly even holding as little as ◇Q-x. On the second round of the suit, declarer is then left with a guess — if West began with ◇Q-x-x-x, he must take a second finesse in order to bring in the suit. However, repeating the finesse will be disastrous when you have ducked your queen. Declarer will then make only one diamond trick!

Once you have gained a reputation of being capable of such ducks, this will be worth tricks in itself! Even when the queen is onside, declarer may be frightened out of a second finesse just because you are sitting East. West will hold ◊Q-x-x-x often enough for this to show a considerable profit.

To cover or not to cover

As beginners, we are all taught to cover an honor with an honor. The more you play, the more you realize that this is not always such a good play. Look at this situation:

```
                ♡ K 10 6 2
              ┌───────────┐
              │     N     │
   ♡ Q 7      │ W       E │      ♡ A 9 3
              │     S     │
              └───────────┘
                ♡ J 8 5 4
```

Cover the jack with the queen, some textbooks will tell you, and you promote partner's nine into a third-round winner. It looks convincing doesn't it? In practice, however, declarer is most unlikely to lead the jack in this position. He would surely lead low to the ten.

When the jack is led, the situation is more likely to be this:

```
                ♡ K 10 6 2
              ┌───────────┐
              │     N     │
   ♡ Q 7      │ W       E │      ♡ 8 5 3
              │     S     │
              └───────────┘
                ♡ A J 9 4
```

Declarer is hoping for a cover if you hold the queen. Produce a casual seven-spot instead and he will rise with dummy's king and finesse on the way back, playing your partner for the queen.

The decision whether or not to cover is often a difficult one. You will not go far wrong by assuming that a good declarer will not lead an honor unless he can afford it to be covered.

The purpose of covering is to promote lower cards in the suit, either in partner's hand or your own. Suppose this is declarer's trump suit and you are sitting East:

```
                ♠ J 3
              ┌───────────┐
              │     N     │
   ♠ 10 8     │ W       E │      ♠ K 9 2
              │     S     │
              └───────────┘
                ♠ A Q 7 6 5 4
```

Declarer has no legitimate way in which to bring home this suit without loss. His only hope is that you do not cover when the jack is led from dummy. Provided you do cover, your nine will score a trick on the third round.

The question of whether or not to cover could take a whole book and we have only a couple of pages available here. As a general rule, you should cover only if there is a chance that you or your partner has some lower card that can be promoted.

To illustrate, here are two examples at opposite ends of the scale.

♡ J 3

♡ ? ? ? N / W E / S ♡ K 7 5 2

♡ ? ? ?

Suppose declarer has shown a six-card heart suit in the auction. When he leads the jack from dummy, should you cover?

To see why doing so is wrong, ask first how many hearts your partner holds. Just one. When, therefore, will it be right to cover the jack with your king?

The answer is 'never'. Indeed, doing so can be spectacularly wrong if partner's singleton is the ace or the queen. Even if partner's heart is a low one, declarer will be unable to set up the suit without conceding a trick to your king. Only by covering do you allow him six heart tricks.

♡ J 4 3

♡ ? ? ? N / W E / S ♡ K 6

♡ ? ? ?

This time, declarer has shown precisely four hearts in the auction. Should you cover when he leads the jack from dummy?

Yes, you should. Indeed, doing so can never cost a trick. If declarer holds ♡ A-Q-10-9, then he was always going to score four tricks in the suit. If his holding is any weaker, you will promote one or more tricks for your partner by covering the jack.

Most situations are less clear-cut. We will offer just one more example. Take a look at this suit from declarer's point of view.

◇ A 8 7 3

◇ ? ? ? N / W E / S ◇ ? ? ?

◇ Q J 9 4

Suppose you lead the queen and West covers with the king. Your best chance is to win the ace and run the eight on the way back. This loses only when West began with precisely ◊K-10 doubleton. (If he had K-10-x you have to lose a trick no matter what you do.)

You can now pick up the suit for no loser if West has covered from ◊K-6, ◊K-5 or ◊K-2. Note how much more difficult things are if the queen wins the trick. Should you lead a low diamond next, hoping that West began with one of the three ◊K-x combinations? Or should you continue with the jack, winning if East started with one of the three ◊10-x holdings? There is no good answer.

It follows that, as a defender, you should usually not cover a queen from the closed hand when you hold ◊K-x or ◊K-x-x. Ducking may leave declarer with a guess on the second round, while covering gives him an easy ride. It's true that you may concede a trick by not covering from K-x if declarer holds only Q-J-x-x (without the ten or nine). With that holding, though, declarer would normally have led towards the queen and jack, catering for king fourth with East.

One of the general guidelines for covering is: do not cover the first of touching honors; cover only when the last of these honors is led. This is easy enough to follow when such as Q-J-9-x is in the dummy (you should not cover the queen on the first round, but cover the jack on the second round). Some defenders find it less easy to visualize the situation when the Q-J-9-x holding is in declarer's hand. It is just the same, really; declarer is most unlikely to lead a queen towards an ace in dummy unless he has at least the jack backing it.

Putting declarer to a guess

In Chapter 4, we examined ways in which declarer could combine his chances — either by taking two finesses or by testing to see whether a suit broke evenly before falling back on a finesse.

Your objective as a defender is to force declarer to a key decision before he has been able to test his options. This deal illustrates the type of position we have in mind:

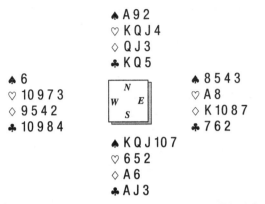

```
              ♠ A 9 2
              ♡ K Q J 4
              ◇ Q J 3
              ♣ K Q 5
♠ 6                        ♠ 8 5 4 3
♡ 10 9 7 3    ┌─────┐     ♡ A 8
◇ 9 5 4 2     │  N  │     ◇ K 10 8 7
♣ 10 9 8 4    │W   E│     ♣ 7 6 2
              │  S  │
              └─────┘
              ♠ K Q J 10 7
              ♡ 6 5 2
              ◇ A 6
              ♣ A J 3
```

Declarer plays in six spades and your partner (West) leads the ♣10. Trumps are drawn in four rounds and declarer then plays a heart to the king. How will you defend?

Suppose you win with the ace and return a passive heart or club. How will the play develop? Declarer will test the heart suit, hoping for a 3-3 break that will allow him to discard his diamond loser. Frustrated in this venture, he will fall back on the diamond finesse. When this succeeds, he will have twelve tricks and his slam.

To give declarer a tougher ride, you must force him to an early decision. Switch to a diamond when you win with the ace of hearts! If declarer finesses now he risks going down when the hearts were 3-3. If he rises with the ace he loses the chance to take a diamond finesse later, if hearts do not divide. On the present deal, declarer is likely to rise with the ◇A. This will bring in the contract not only when hearts are 3-3 but also when West holds four hearts and the ◇K (he will be squeezed when declarer cashes his last black-suit winner).

Whether or not declarer is likely to take any particular losing option that you present him, it is better to try your luck in that direction, rather than sitting back and accepting your fate.

Here is a more difficult deal on the same theme:

```
                    ♠ K Q 10 2
                    ♡ 9 6 3
                    ◇ A J 3
                    ♣ Q 5 2
    ♠ 8 6 4            ┌─────────┐        ♠ 7 5
    ♡ K Q J 4          │    N    │        ♡ A 10 8 2
    ◇ 10 9 7           │ W     E │        ◇ Q 8 6 4
    ♣ A 9 3            │    S    │        ♣ 10 8 6
                       └─────────┘
                    ♠ A J 9 3
                    ♡ 7 5
                    ◇ K 5 2
                    ♣ K J 7 4
```

Playing in 4♠, declarer ruffed the third heart, drew trumps, and played on clubs. They broke 3-3, he was pleased to see, so he was able to discard a diamond from dummy. A diamond ruff gave him ten tricks.

What could the defenders have done? If they were playing the signaling method that we recommended in *Defensive Signaling* (Book 8 of this series), East would play high-low on the first two hearts, showing four cards in the suit. Knowing that there were no more heart tricks to come, West might have switched to the ◇10. Declarer would win with the king, draw trumps, and play on clubs. When West won the second round, he could play another diamond, forcing declarer to a decision on the diamond finesse before he knew if the clubs were 3-3.

If declarer gets two bites of every cherry, he will be successful more regularly. Your objective, therefore, is to force him into a decision before he knows what is happening. There is little more satisfying in this game than to present declarer with a losing option and then watch him take it to go down in a contract that could have been made.

Key points

1. Withholding your high cards, allowing declarer to think his finesses are winning when they are not, may give him a losing option.

2. Another useful tactic is to force declarer to guess whether to take a finesse before he knows how many tricks he needs from the suit.

3. Should you cover an honor with an honor? It is usually right to cover if your partner may have a holding that can be promoted. When declarer leads touching honors, though, it usually best to cover only the last one.

A.

♠ Q 7 6
♡ A
♢ A K 7 6
♣ A K 9 3 2

♡ Q led

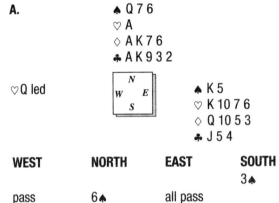

♠ K 5
♡ K 10 7 6
♢ Q 10 5 3
♣ J 5 4

WEST	NORTH	EAST	SOUTH
			3♠
pass	6♠	all pass	

West, your partner, leads the queen of hearts against a small slam in spades. Declarer wins with dummy's ace and leads the queen of spades. Do you cover? What is the purpose of your chosen play?

B.

♠ Q 4
♡ K Q 3
♢ J 10
♣ A K J 8 6 3

♠ J led

♠ 8 3
♡ A J 9 5
♢ K 9 8 4
♣ 9 5 2

WEST	NORTH	EAST	SOUTH
			1NT (15-17)
pass	6NT	all pass	

Declarer wins partner's spade lead with dummy's queen, crosses to the ♣Q, and plays a heart to the king. Plan the defense.

Answers

A. You should not cover with the king, since it is extremely unlikely that this can promote a trick for your partner. Covering with the king can cost in two different ways. Suppose declarer's trumps are A-J-10-x-x-x. If you produce a smooth low card on the queen, he may conclude that you cannot hold the king. In that case he may rise with the ace, hoping to drop a singleton king from West. Another possibility is that South holds J-10-9-x-x-x in the trump suit. Cover the queen now and the trick will be completed by your partner's bare ace. Who will you play the rest of the session with then?

B. You can count declarer for nine top tricks in the black suits. He therefore needs only three red-suit tricks for his contract. Suppose you capture the king of hearts with the ace and switch to diamonds. Declarer will know that he needs a successful diamond finesse to make the slam. He will put in the queen of diamonds (which you know he has, from a count of the outstanding points) and soon have twelve tricks before him. See the difference if you coolly allow dummy's king of hearts to win the trick. Declarer will then have to guess whether to play a second heart to the queen, playing West for the heart ace, or to risk everything on the diamond finesse. Since many Easts would have grabbed their ace at the first opportunity, he is quite likely to get it wrong and play a second heart. You will then score two heart tricks to beat the slam. Partner will definitely finish the session with you after that!